Pebbles and Stones

the rough and smooth edges of life...

Joy Kar

To my family and friends, whose love and support have been the rhythm to my words,

to the muses who whispered in my ear,

and to the fragments of my soul, now woven into these pages,

may they find a home in the hearts of those who read them.

This collection is dedicated with gratitude and love.

Acknowledgement

This is a list that I wish never ends....!
I am deeply grateful
-to my family, who have been my rock, my safe haven, and my constant source of inspiration–thank you for your unconditional love and encouragement.
- to my friends for their unwavering support and encouragement throughout this journey.
-And to the muses, who whispered in my ear and nudged me to keep writing – may these poems honor your whispers.

Preface

In the tapestry of life, we find ourselves navigating a landscape of contrasts – rough edges that test our resilience, and smooth, rounded surfaces that soothe our souls. *Pebbles and Stones* is a collection of poems that explores this intricate dance between the jagged, turbulent, and the serene.

These poems are fragments of my own journey, gathered from the depths of joy, sorrow, love, and loss. They are an attempt to make sense of the world around me, to find meaning in the quirky and the smooth, and to hold onto hope when darkness descends.

I invite you to walk with me along the winding paths of human experience. Let us pick up the pebbles of memory and turn the stones over, revealing the hidden truths within.

May these poems be a reminder that even in the roughest of times, there is beauty to be found, and that even in the smoothest of moments, there is depth to be explored.

As you read these pages, I hope you will find echoes of your own story, resonances that speak to your own struggles and triumphs. For in the end, it is not the pebbles or stones that define us, but the spaces between – the silences, the whispers, and the unspoken words.

Thank you for joining me on this journey.

— Joy Kar

1. Plume

Plume was happy in her world.
Netted and strong.
Safe.
Chirping, preening and pecking.
Till one day –
the maid left her seed bowl full
and
her latch open.

Plume fluttered away.
Not very far.
She had learnt to flutter, not fly.
Resting on a branch
and with no food,
She became fodder for the crow and the cat.

Next time I will give Plume –
Cage-born that she is –
A bigger netted world.

She won't flutter....but fly.
Back to me!

2. The Chase

Chasing butterflies is fun.
Success is funnier.
The green lawns laced in dew
The warm gold bathes the blooms –
To esoteric heights.
The flitting colours adding to the excitement
Some simply run around.
Seeing the flowers and catching their breath,
Only to pry on them –
Again. And again.
Others run from one meadow to the other
Savouring the smell
And sounds of nature and power.

Chasing butterflies is fun.
Success funnier.
To catch them,
You need a net
First.

3. Friends

My friends are
the touch-me-not plant.
Few and not easy to find.
Folding up at the slightest touch!

My friends are resplendent
Flowering in the cool air and sun
And so much fun

My friends are camphor
Evaporating when left alone.
Adding the paleful glow
When the arati of the famous flow

My friends are eucalyptus
Standing tall
Surviving the barren land
Sucking the water from the dry rocks
Fragrance in the molten air

My friends are mine
Exploding in war.
And wrapped softly in peace.

4. Teacher

The old haggard teacher taught—
Taught well.
Some he loved more
Coz they studied more
Even after the bell.

He taught best
And most won the test
They learned
their muscle mass strong and taut.

Moved on giving pleasure
to the unread and the naïve
bathed in the glory of their deeds.

The teacher is now old
and blind.
He hears the tinkling glasses
He hears the titter and sighs
Of those who loved so much more..
The distant school bell —
He was never deaf.

None to read him the lessons
he taught so well.
In his memory
They smiled
and presented him a book in Braille.

5. Is it Over...

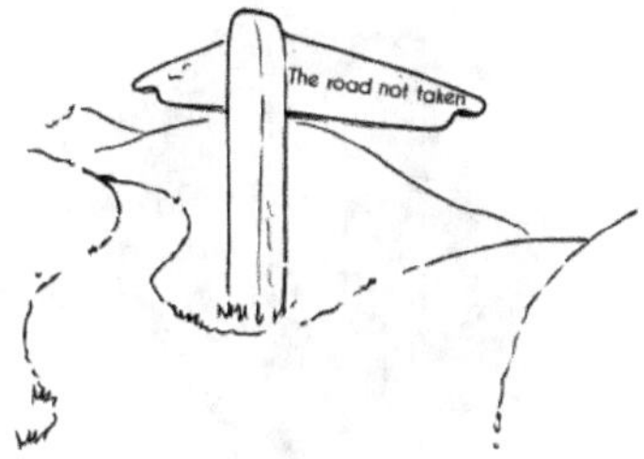

After six it's over.
After four it's over.
For some!

After ninety minutes it's over.
After eighteen holes it's over.
When December 31 comes it's over.
Again.
When the gavel falls it's over.

The gravel finally comes over.
The ashes strewn over the holy waters.
It's the end
not over.

Next time when you say it's over, think.
Is it the end? Or over?
For the next?

6. Lie

Lie well.
On firm beds.
If you have a bad back.
Lie well.
After a hard day's labour.
Without fear or favour
Lie well.
When the storms gather around
with fury and sound
when missiles fly.
Lie well.

Lest the truth engulfs.
Or truth consumes
Or the truth consummates.
Lie well!

7. Every drop

Flood waters swirl in
a dance of destruction.
The barren Thar, every drop a nectar.
In a senseless war
every drop expendable.
In the OT every drop counts.
Factories spew out vials,
yet another inventory
Saving a life,
every drop a saviour.

the cacophony of laughter
and revelry
spewing tears of joy
be it in pain and hurt,
every drop counts!

Every drop is gold.
Warm or cold
Save them!

8. Lame Bull

The lame old bull smiles,
watching the prancing kids.
Once revered in temples,
now scavenges in the market dump.

There are some kids who come
and indulge him –
with a wag of his tail
the kids swagger without fail.
the horns stand guard
Momentary
briefly..for a moment.

The old, lame one
benign and wry
looks on
Two kids enjoy better.
Playing.
Than
with a lame old bull.

9. Stop

When I asked you
to stop,
I meant —
you stop because I want to move ahead.
you stop because there is danger ahead
and I care for you.
you stop because someone else has to move
ahead
and I want him to.

Or enough!
a new year, a new day, a new month begins.
to start and
to Stop.

10. Show You

What you face
depends on what you want to show.
The veil of the wit
the wail of the fear
hidden by the cunning and the sweet.
You don't go far!
as you walk alone.

The fool in me
manage to stumble and fall
confusing the immature mind
into indiscretion.
platitudes raining on misty hearts.

What we show is not
in the rags we bind ourselves in
Not in the laces that we engulf in
but
wrapped in the words and unplanned touches
transmitting messages
for a lifetime!

11. Don't swim with me

The first time
my throat went dry
The next time too.

I have learnt to read
the tide and swim
the ghastly current
I have learnt to read
Every moment when
the heart ached in revolt.

I have swum the seas
Gently treading the sand
Under the azure sky
The blue, blue sky.

Don't swim with me.
Would you want to be wet?
Under the blue sky.

Sun and the moon
separate us.
Mind and our hearts
separate us.
Morals and principles. Remain different.
Separate us.
Say not it's black. Or white. Or grey.
Older flowers fade earlier than the buds yet
to bloom.

Only orchids remain longer.
But then, they are rare and special.

12. Crowing

the doves were docile
the sparrows shrieked
the hawks swooped
and the koel had fun.

laid her eggs in the crow's nest
despite gnarled limbs and crow's feet.
the love to start our own
protecting from the hawks, vultures and
serpents.

Does the crow know this?
Or is it human like us?

13. The call back

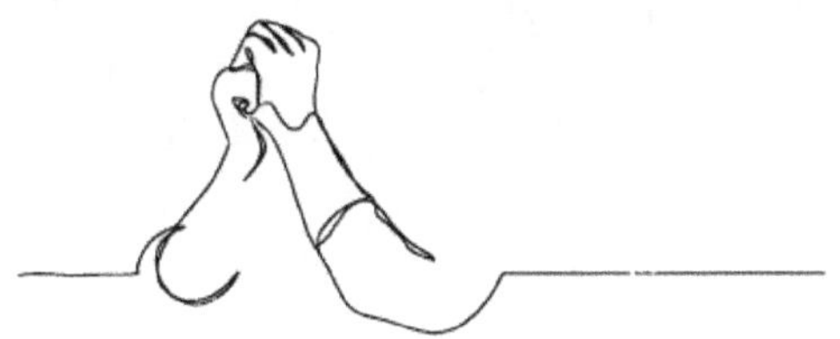

"I'll call you back."
And no response.
my sms.
And no reply.
A call.
Which keeps ringing on.

Times have changed and you should know.
The appraisal form
not in your grip
The appointment letter
not for you to sign.
the tired limbs of mine.
The revenue I don't bring,
or earn.

Birds eat seeds.
And hyenas carrion.
Wake up before
the long night begins!

14. Walk, don't fly

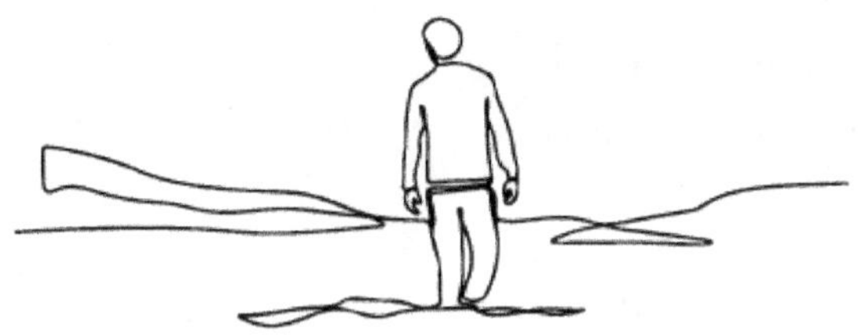

He said he loved pink,
he didn't know that he loved violet.
When she wore blue
not knowing she preferred
the azure.
Entrapped in the maze
So often,
we want to fly
when we are made to walk.
To keep pace with the old and infirm.
Only to move on
for luck and company
handling the infirm hands.

Wear the blue.
Fly.
Or walk.
To touch. To feel.
And not just hold
the old and infirm.

15. Fruits

Sweetest fruits take the longest
to ripen.
The forbidden fruit, a myth.

Tailored to ensure that I eat
and not you.
Poison fruits even birds don't touch!
the fruits of labour best shared
with those who care
no other maze to explore
in the cavernous orchards.

Some share more.
But you get less!

16. I do

I love compliments.
I do.
my attire, looks and me as a person.
I love attention.
I do.
By being nice, laughing, smiling, toying with
my fingers
I wear a tear drop or two
that makes more protective of me and more.
Who doesn't?
I do.

17. and I smiled

I threw the first pebble in the pond,
the ripple
creating lovely rings in the water.

A young boy, I fought –
and lost.
It hurt
When the rock was thrown at me.
It pained
When I could not see.

And grown up now,
it hurt, when papers were thrown at me.
For a shoddy job that I couldn't foresee.

When the metal band struck
the strings of a crescendo
It didn't hurt.
It pained.
And I smiled...

18. Saying No

As children we said yes.
Had to.
Agree.
Be it for soup, veggies or studies.
Innocence made us agree
to haircuts and nail clips!
In love we said yes
to the first demure smile.
Older now – stronger and infirm
Currency life wallets are networked
now.
Making us resilient
To say No.
Now.
It's important. To say no and hear no.
If only to realise the value of yes!
I do.
Do you?

19. Lose it

To lose a ring makes me sad
To lose a call gets me worried
Losing money makes me poor
Losing a client brands me inefficient
Losing a friend makes me distressed
But when I lose my blood
I know it's time to test
Coz it must be my illness
And wait for the report
And the doctor.

20. The rest is destiny

A fifth of an iceberg seen
The balance lurks
the chilling, swirling salt sea underneath.
Silent.
Regal yet sinister.
A fifth of a cube settles
easily in the tall single malt.
Chilling the swirling emotions contained
beneath.
Regal. Yet heady.
How many Titanics do we see?
In disaster or in the dance of life?
the iceberg or the ice cube.
Both float with a fifth for all to see.
The rest is destiny.

21. There is life...

There is life after life.
There is life after death.
Subtlety – a state of mind
Some achieve
feeding crumbs to the pigeon.
Some don't
hogging headlines and airwaves
or sending millions to Auschwitz.

A good heart may have weak valves.
But it still is good.
There is life after life.
For some
Who are born to die –

Warm, generous, and trusting
And for some
who die to be born again
to escape
The treachery of daily life!

22. Smoke in Bhopal

One winter night of smoke
Ensured tears – till today.

We are smoke.
Sweet, Soothing, Cloying
and Clawing.

Noxious
and obnoxious.
Useful and Useless.

Swirling and twirling
in an all-important frenzy.
Until one day –
there is a sudden gust.
The smoke vanishes into thin air.

I hear,
'Where there is smoke, there must be fire'.

23. Pores

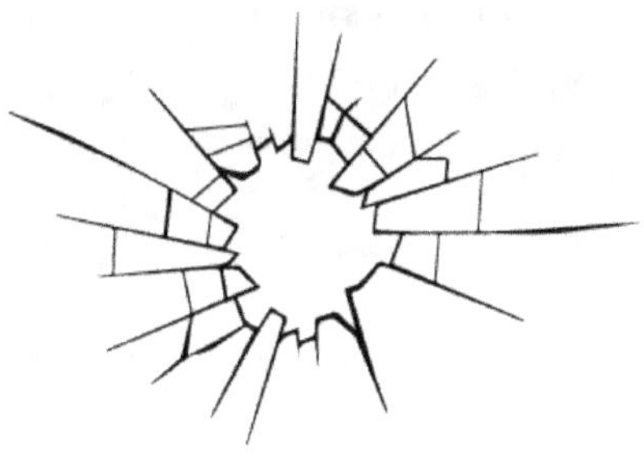

Watching my beads
Of perspiration
Oozing pore by pore...
My body exults
As the warm and humid sun caresses
Me and my browned limbs

I have savoured
Happiness and success
Pore by pore.
Pored over glory, pored over humility
And pored over pages
Of destiny

Too much, too soon
Too fast
And I break out in a sweat!
Let me perspire, then
Pore by pore.

24. Mystery

Life is a mystery
So is love and God
a mystery.

I filled the goblet
The glasses and the tea cups
Till they flowed over.

I absorbed the pungent, the sweet
And the heady
Swirled in the fumes of it
And yet broke out in a sweat.

I immersed myself
In the innate and the deep
Rejoiced in the happiness within
Yet my thirst
My mind remained
Incomplete.

I have been filling
The cup from the ocean
The depth unknown
The grainy sand
Yet the taste remains
A conjecture.

25. Truth

There is truth in rubbish
Grotesque and stink
There is truth in messages
In words that sting
There is truth in rumors
In encryptions deciphered.

But, there remains the *but* ....

There is truth in our hearts –
silent, loyal and firm.
A truth so fresh, fragrant
and beautiful!

9 789363 304581